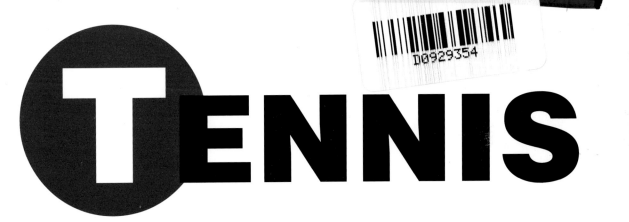

# TENNIS

**W**RITTEN BY ELIZABETH SIRIMARCO

**ROURKE CORPORATION, INC.**
VERO BEACH, FLORIDA 32964

**PRO-AM
SPORTS**

The Rourke Corporation, Inc.
P.O. Box 3328, Vero Beach, FL 32964

Sirimarco, Elizabeth 1966—
     Tennis / by Elizabeth Sirimarco.
        p.  cm. — (Pro-am sports)
     Includes bibliographical references (p. 47)
     ISBN 0-86593-343-X
     1.  Tennis—Juvenile literature.  I. Title.  II. Series.
GV996.5.S57  1993
     796.342—dc20                                          93-27152
                                                           CIP
                                                           AC

Cover photograph:  Allsport (Bob Martin)
Allsport USA 4, 6, 39 (Simon Bruty); 8 (Chris Raphael);
     12 (Chris Cole); 14 (Gary M. Prior); 15, 40 (Richard
     Martin/Agence Vandystadt); 19, 33 (Yanh
     Guichaoua/Agence Vandystadt); 20 (Tony Duffy);
     22 (Nathan Bilow); 23 (Bernard Giani/Agence
     Vandystadt); 26, 32 (Bob Martin); 27 (Don Smith);
     35 (David Cannon)
ATP/Russ Adams Productions 11, 28, 36
Colorado Tennis Association 30, 42

Series Editor:  Gregory Lee
Book design and production:
     The Creative Spark, San Clemente, CA

30033001309561

*A sport once played by French royalty becomes one of the most popular and exciting games of individual skill and style.*

# CONTENTS

CHAPTER ONE

**T**ennis Anyone? ........................ **5**

CHAPTER TWO

**G**etting Started ........................ **15**

CHAPTER THREE

**P**laying the Game ........................ **23**

CHAPTER FOUR

**W**hat Does It Take? ........................ **35**

CHAPTER FIVE

**G**etting Involved ........................ **41**

*Glossary* **45**

*For Additional Information* **47**

*Index* **48**

**HOT TIP:**
*A racket is not just a racket. To learn how to choose the proper one for you, turn to page 19.*

**T**ennis is a supreme blend of grace and athletic ability. Form, concentration, and strength must be combined to make a winner.

# Tennis Anyone?

**CHAPTER ONE**

**W**hat is it that has made the game of tennis so popular in countries all around the world? Why is it a favorite sport among both children and adults, men and women alike? Some tennis players are professionals who make a lot of money playing a sport they love, but most are amateurs—fans who pick up a racket on the weekend or after school. Many of these "weekend pros" are so dedicated to the game that they are champions in their own right, playing tough matches and winning amateur tournaments with their fine-tuned skills.

Tennis is a sport for the individual. Unlike soccer or softball, sports in which a player is part of a team, tennis enthusiasts must rely on their own skills to win a match. The individual's skills are vital to the outcome of the match in both singles and doubles tennis. There is no room for a "weak link," and there are no strong teammates to help the weak ones. In other words, when a tennis player loses, there is no one else to blame. More importantly, when a player wins, he or she gets all the credit! Maybe that's what makes the sport such a challenge.

Tennis is an easy sport for most people to learn. Nearly every community has classes that teach the basics of the sport, and many students are introduced to the game in physical education classes at school. Players do not need to travel to find a place to play, as skiers must to find the slopes—tennis courts are available to fans of the game in cities and towns all around the world. Players do not need to round up six or seven teammates to get a game going; a worthy opponent is all that's necessary. Equipment, like rackets and balls, can be purchased at reasonable prices, and many communities have free courts on which to play. The only things a person needs to become a good player are interest, motivation, and practice.

Being young doesn't necessarily mean being inexperienced. Monica Seles was an international champion before her 20th birthday.

How old do you have to be to start playing the game? If the big professional tournaments are any indication, starting young is an important part of the recipe for tennis success. The players who win seem to be younger and younger each year. Many must have started playing shortly after they learned to walk! Take a look at Monica Seles, for example. At age 19, she had won eight major championship titles. In 1989, 17-year-old Michael Chang became the first American to win the French Open in more than 30 years.

In the hope of following in the footsteps of a favorite pro, children have started picking up the game at a young age, developing a mean serve and a competitive spirit. It is becoming more and more common to see youngsters who play such a tough game that they are able to beat their parents or older brothers and sisters with little effort. Whether their goal is to play in tournaments, to join a school team, or just to get some exercise and have fun doing it, tennis is a favorite sport of many people, young and old alike.

## A Little Background

Tennis players today wear specially designed shoes and use "high-tech" rackets that are said to help them win. Television airs the big professional tournaments via satellite to millions of people in countries all over the world. It may seem as though tennis is a very modern sport, but it has actually been around for centuries. However, early forms of the game were quite different from what we now recognize as tennis.

For example, it wasn't until about 200 years ago that tennis was first played outdoors. Before that, indoor courts were used to play a French game called *jeu de paume*. This game was played in monasteries during the eleventh century—an interesting start for the sport. Imagine the monks wearing their long, serious tunics while playing the fast-paced games of today! More than just the attire was different. The rackets had no strings and solid faces, probably a lot like what is used today in the game of paddle ball. It wasn't until the fifteenth century that an Italian priest introduced the first strung racket.

The sport became popular among a small sector of the European population: royalty. As a result, it became known as *royal tennis*. Where did the word "tennis" come from? *Tenez* is an old French word that means "look out!" In royal tennis, the server would shout "Tenez!" to an opponent as the ball was struck.

Much like today's racquetball, players of royal tennis used not only the court, but the walls surrounding it as well. Imagine the way it might have looked. Players were dressed in elaborate outfits, specially designed for the game. A number of servants were on hand to fetch the ball, tend to mild injuries, dab away perspiration, or offer refreshments. A servant even tossed the ball up for the player to serve, which is why we call the opening motion of each point a *service*. A round of royal tennis probably wasn't quite as intense as the exciting matches we see today!

In the 1800s, ordinary people finally began to play the game outdoors. Players no longer needed to be wealthy to afford an indoor court, and the common folk were able to take part. It was then that the sport became more popular, and this form of the game is much closer to what we now call tennis. In 1873, a British major named Walter

**The grass courts of Wimbledon, site of the world's most famous tennis tournament. That's two-time winner Boris Becker taking a dive.**

Clopton Wingfield introduced a new game at a lawn party in Wales. He called it *Sphairistiké*, or "sticky." The game was an immediate success, but Wingfield's strange choice for a name didn't catch on. In no time at all, people were calling the sport *lawn tennis* because it was played on a court made of grass. Although Americans simply call the game tennis, the British still use the original name.

Even in its early days, lawn tennis could be played by both men and women, which increased its popularity. Sporting clubs began to include it in their offerings: the All-England Croquet Club became the All-England Croquet and Lawn Tennis Club. In 1877, this club began to sponsor an annual tournament called The Championships in Lawn Tennis. Today, the tournament is most often called by its nickname, *Wimbledon*. It is still one of the most important professional tennis tournaments anywhere—and one of the world's favorite sporting events.

By this time, the sport had also become popular across the Atlantic Ocean in the United States. Legend has it that an American woman who visited the British territory of Bermuda brought tennis rackets back to the United States and introduced the game. It caught on quickly, and the rest is history.

## Setting the Standards

Players on both sides of the Atlantic played the sport in a pretty relaxed style until 1880, when standards for some of the equipment and the court's measurements were established. In 1881, the *United States Tennis Association* (USTA) was born. Today, this American organization still works to promote amateur tennis and make sure the rules of the game are upheld.

In no time, matches were taking place between the United Kingdom and the United States. The popularity of the international tournaments led to the founding of the *Davis Cup*, today's most important team event. The very first Davis Cup featured only the Americans competing against the British. Things have changed, and today players from countries around the world take part in the event, which was named after the first winning team captain, American Dwight F. Davis.

## The Challenge

For about 50 years, the big tennis tournaments were played on a challenge basis. This means that the defending champion always played in the final match of the tournament; in other words, he or she had to play only one match to keep the championship title. The challenger had to beat many other players in order to reach the finals and win the right to play the champion. As a result, the well-rested champ, who had been under little stress during the tournament, was often difficult to beat.

In 1922, Wimbledon stopped using the challenge tournament system and switched to a "knock-out tournament." Defending champions had to prove their superiority by beating a series of opponents in each tournament. If a player lost a match, he was out of the tournament—players now had to win their way to the finals. This allowed many new players to become fierce competitors. The French surfaced as very tough competition; four men in particular began to dominate the game, both in France and abroad. Jean Borotra, Henri Cochet, Rene Lacoste, and Jacques Brugnon won the Wimbledon men's singles title six times in the first eight years after the challenge system was removed. The quartet was known as the Four Musketeers, and today the trophy awarded at the French Open bears that nickname in their honor.

Along with Wimbledon, other important international tennis events began to make the news. The United States and Australia started their own international tournaments (now called the U.S. Open and the Australian

Open). France expanded its championship to include players from other countries in 1925. Today these four championships are the most important tournaments for professional tennis players. Winning all four in a single year means that a person has achieved a *Grand Slam*—still the highest honor and most difficult achievement in the game. Only two men (American Don Budge and Australian Rod Laver) and two women (American Maureen O'Connolly and Britisher Margaret Court) have accomplished this tremendous feat.

## Open Tournaments

Tennis first came to the world's attention as an amateur sport. The best players had to be content with a trophy and the knowledge that they were among the toughest competitors in the world. Things have certainly changed. For today's top professionals, tennis is a well-paid, full-time job. The best pros earn a great deal of money playing their sport. For example, top-ranked Monica Seles earned nearly $2.5 million in 1991; Stefan Edberg earned about $2.3 million that same year. In addition, many of today's players "go pro" at an early age. Jennifer Capriati, for example, played in her first professional tournament at age 13.

It is difficult to imagine a time when competitors were involved "just for the sport of it," but in the early days, that is exactly how it was. From the very first Wimbledon championship in 1877 until 1968, all the players in the big tournaments were *amateurs*, people who were not paid to play the sport. Those who played for money, called *professionals*, could not play in the same tournaments as the amateurs, and the most prestigious championships were all amateur events.

Professional tennis got its start in 1926, when French star Suzanne Lenglen was paid a hefty $50,000 to tour the world and display her talent. This meant that one of the great stars of the court could no longer participate in the most important—or amateur—tournaments. As time went on, playing for money began to lure more and more players away from their amateur status. In the 1950s and '60s, many top players began making money on increasingly popular professional tours. Fans of the sport worried that the game was no longer as competitive as it once was and that the professional circuit was pulling too many good players away from amateur play. Since the professionals were unable to compete in the all-important Grand Slam events,

**Michael Chang became the first American to win the French Open in more than three decades.**

**The hair, the clothing, and the attitude of Andre Agassi bring a world of colorful changes to pro tennis.**

tennis finally went "open" in 1968. Both amateurs and professionals could now compete.

While today's most famous events may only be for professionals, amateurs still have many opportunities to compete in tournaments. Tennis players at all levels of play find a challenge—and have fun—playing tournaments sponsored by the USTA or their local tennis club. Events are held for both beginners and advanced players, and children and adults each have a wide variety of tournaments to choose from each year. Perhaps one of the best things about the sport is that almost anyone can learn to play, and once a player becomes good enough, it's easy to find competition to show off his or her skills.

## A New Image

In years past, tennis was a very conservative sport with specific rules of etiquette, meaning that players had to behave and dress in a certain way when on the court. Today, young players have brought a youthful, spirited feeling to the sport.

Stars like Monica Seles and Andre Agassi play by the rules, but each has brought a unique style to the game. Seles, a tough competitor who won her first professional tournament in her early teens, is known for the loud yelps she makes each time she hits the ball. Agassi broke the game's traditional dress code by sporting an earring and wild, colorful clothing. Frenchman Yannick Noah has even worn dread locks on the court!

Tennis may have been around for a while, but the sport's new youthful image has changed the game in recent years. The rules may be the same, but what was once the sport of royalty is now a sport for everyone. As tennis has become more free-spirited, many young people have decided to give the game a try.

Players of all ages have found that the sport is also a fun way to exercise. More than just competition, tennis is an opportunity to have fun while getting a great workout. Says one young tennis fan, "I don't play on a team or anything, but my friends and I have a lot of fun hitting the ball around. Sometimes we stay out on the court for three or four hours, running around and practicing our shots."

Whether you've set your sights on a career in tennis, want to play for a local team, or simply want to play for fun, the opportunities are there for you. Once you've mastered the basics, you can bring your own style and strengths to the game. That is what has made tennis so much fun—for players and spectators alike—over the years.

**T**ennis is played on a variety of court surfaces. Clay and asphalt are the most common in North America.

# Getting Started

### CHAPTER TWO

**I**f you've ever watched tennis on television or played a little yourself, you may be familiar with the different kinds of equipment one needs to play the game. Nonetheless, there are a lot of different choices you can make, from the shape of your racket to the look of your shoes to the kind of court on which you will play.

In North America, cement courts are the most common, particularly in the western states. There are many other types as well, constructed of grass, sand, clay, asphalt, and shale. Indoor courts are often made of wood, carpet, or rubber, but these materials do not weather well outside.

The different kinds of court surfaces affect the way the ball bounces, and the best players must be able to adjust their game to the surface. Many amateurs play on only one type of court, but as they become more advanced, they must learn the techniques necessary for play on other surfaces.

**Although pro tennis players must learn to play well on all surfaces, most will admit to preferring one over another.**

What is the major difference between the various types of court surface? "Fast" or "hard" courts are those on which the ball bounces low and fast. These include grass, cement, some carpet courts, and artificial grass. With less time to make the shots, players who are used to "slow" or "soft" courts (clay, asphalt, and rubber) often have a tough time on hard, fast courts. Likewise, players who are accustomed to fast courts have trouble with the slower and steep-angled bounce of the slow courts.

Top player Pete Sampras comes from California, where there are no clay courts. He has a tough time at the French Open because he isn't at his best on clay. At the same event in 1993, Spaniard Sergi Bruguera was able to use the clay surface to his advantage when he upset the world's number two player, Jim Courier, in a tough, five-set match. Ivan Lendl, considered the best male player throughout much of the 1980s, has won many tournaments. The grass courts at Wimbledon seem to cause him problems, however, and he has never been able to win at "The Championships."

No matter what the surface, today's tennis court is always rectangular in shape. This was not always the case. When Major Clopton Wingfield first introduced the game of "sticky," the court was shaped like an hourglass, and the net

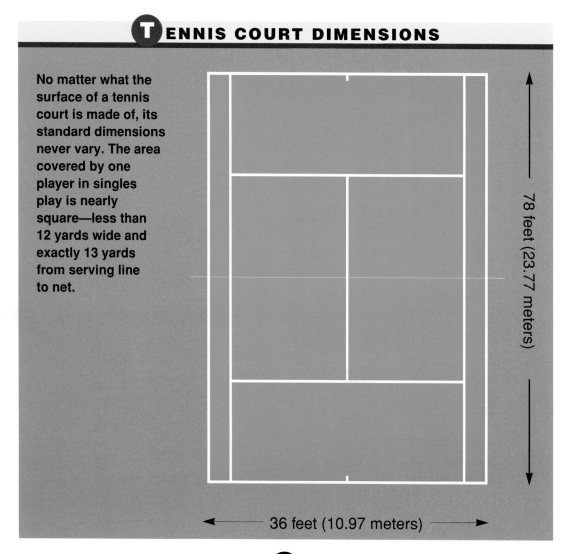

## TENNIS COURT DIMENSIONS

No matter what the surface of a tennis court is made of, its standard dimensions never vary. The area covered by one player in singles play is nearly square—less than 12 yards wide and exactly 13 yards from serving line to net.

78 feet (23.77 meters)

36 feet (10.97 meters)

was placed at the narrowest part. The rectangular shape of the tennis court has remained unchanged for about 100 years.

Tennis courts must always be the same size: 78 feet (23.77 meters) in length by 36 feet (10.97 meters) in width. The court is divided in two by a net, and there are markings in various places to show where the boundaries are for singles and doubles games, where the serve must go, and so on.

Boundary lines are painted around the limits of the court in the shape of a rectangle. The lines at the sides are called *sidelines,* while the lines at the ends are called *baselines.* Perpendicular to the sidelines are the *tramlines,* which are the sidelines for *singles* play; that is, any ball that falls beyond the tramline or the baseline in a singles match is called "out." The area between the sidelines and the tramlines is used only in *doubles* play; that is, any ball that bounces beyond the sideline or the baseline is called "out."

## INBOUND PLAYING AREAS

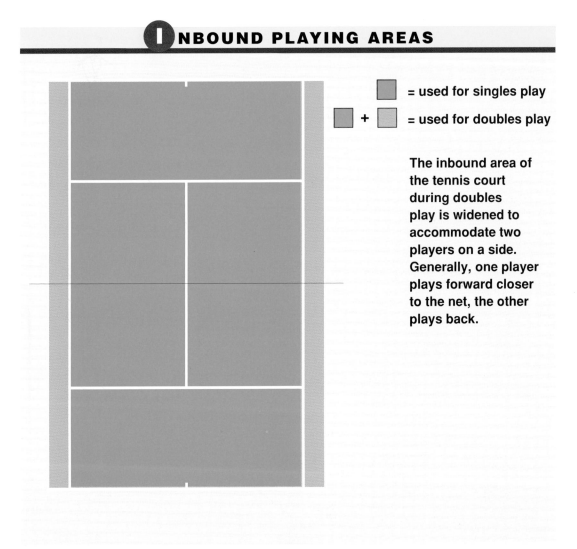

= used for singles play

+ = used for doubles play

The inbound area of the tennis court during doubles play is widened to accommodate two players on a side. Generally, one player plays forward closer to the net, the other plays back.

The net that divides the court in half must be three feet high at the center. Sometimes players will check the height of the net by standing a racket on end and the head of another on top of it at a right angle. This isn't an accurate measure, but it does show if the net is significantly higher or lower than it ought to be. On the posts that hold the net are handles that can be used to adjust the net.

There are other lines on the court as well. The service line runs parallel to the baseline but does not extend beyond the tramlines. Another line, called the center service line, is placed from the center of the net to the center of the service line. The last court marking rests at the middle of the baseline and is called the center mark. As with the rest of the court, all of these lines must be at precisely measured points.

## The Racket

Rackets were traditionally made out of wood, but today's fancier versions are made of many different materials, including aluminum, graphite, and fiberglas. In addition, the head of the racket (the part that makes contact with the ball) used to be much smaller than what we see today. Over the years, rackets have been made in a variety of shapes and sizes, as manufacturers tried to discover new ways to improve a player's game. Many people believe the new rackets have made a big difference in the sport, as they give players more power and control.

For many years, there were no rules about racket design. As manufacturers began to experiment with size and shape, however, tennis officials decided it would be wise to have a set of guidelines. Today, the tennis racket has a set of precise measurements. For example, the length of the handle must not exceed 32 inches, and the racket itself can be no more than 12.5 inches wide.

The hitting area, or the *face* of the racket, must be flat and made from a pattern of crossed strings that connect to the racket frame. The strings are made of natural gut or artificial materials like nylon. The central part of the strung area is called the "sweet spot," and it is the best place to hit the ball because it results in a controlled, solid return.

Rackets can be strung at different tensions for different kinds of players. For example, a tightly strung racket offers more power but less control, so beginners usually start with looser strings. A more advanced competitor, who plays an offensive, serve-and-volley game, may prefer tighter strings.

**The racket is more than just your equipment—it's your partner. Jennifer Capriati has dropped hers after a tough rally.**

Is the kind of racket you use that important? Most advanced players will say it is, but a beginner need not buy the best, most expensive racket made. While learning the basics, it is enough to have a solid, well-strung racket that is comfortable for the player to use.

Rackets also come in different weights, and a player should select what is right for him or her. Try a few practice strokes. If the racket feels too heavy, it isn't right for you. The size of the grip (or handle) is important, too. If the grip is too big, it will slip in your hand. If it is too small, it will cause cramps. A knowledgeable salesperson at a sporting goods store will help a beginning player select the right racket.

## The Ball

In the early days of tennis, the balls were always white, but many players thought the color made them difficult to see. Today, most players use bright yellow balls. Some balls designed for night play are neon orange.

Tennis balls are made of rubber that is covered with wool or an artificial substitute. Special equipment is used to pressurize the ball, meaning that air is sealed inside it so it will bounce. There are even rules about how high a ball must bounce. When dropped to a concrete surface from a height of 100 inches, a tennis ball must bounce between 53 and 58 inches.

In professional tournaments, balls lose their pressure quickly because air escapes when they are hit repeatedly. As small amounts of air escape, the ball must be hit harder and harder to achieve the same results as when hitting a new ball. To combat this problem, tournament balls are replaced at the end of the first seven games, then every nine after that. The average player does not damage the ball as quickly as a pro. Nonetheless, it's important for players of all levels to use new balls with good bounce, otherwise they will have to work harder to hit good shots.

**Beginning and advanced players alike should always wear comfortable clothing when playing tennis.**

## Clothing

The strict dress code that once was an important part of the game has changed over the years. In tournament play, white was once considered the only appropriate color for tennis attire. Today, colors and prints are popular on the tennis court. Nonetheless, the rules at Wimbledon, as well as at some other tennis clubs, still require that shirts, shorts, and skirts be primarily white.

Comfort is the most important consideration when choosing clothing for tennis. A good pair of shoes protects the feet from constant impact on a hard surface. They should be lightweight and offer support—features that can help prevent injury. Likewise, clothing that allows the player to move easily and stay cool is essential.

How important are all of these things? Will the right racket or the right clothing make that much of a difference? Many experts say they will. If your shoes give you blisters, you certainly will not play your best game. If your racket's grip is the wrong size, you'll have problems as well. If your clothes are too tight or too hot, the discomfort will affect your game. Tennis players do not have to spend a fortune to be outfitted for the game, but a few essentials can make a big difference in your play.

**T**he serve puts the ball in play. Many games are decided at this crucial moment.

# Playing the Game

## CHAPTER THREE

**T**he object of tennis is to win *rallies*, the sequence of shots made by players hitting the ball back and forth to each other. If you have ever seen a really great tennis match, you know that rallies can go on for a long time. Two good players can return a lot of difficult shots before one of them wins the point. It is a lot of work, but oddly enough, the word rally comes from the French word for rest or revive. When the the players of royal tennis kept the ball in play for a while, the servants were able to rest, and that's how the word rally came to be used.

To win a point, a tennis player tries to hit the ball in a way that his or her opponent cannot successfully return it. One way is to hit it in such a way that it travels too fast or out of reach. When the opponent returns the ball and it is either out of bounds or into the net, this is called an *unforced error*. The player has made an avoidable mistake.

**Good players often practice their serve more than any other aspect of their game.**

Each point starts with the service or *serve*, the only tennis stroke in which a player has complete control. The first player to serve is determined by a coin toss, or by spinning a racket. The winner opens the first game by serving, then the players alternate serving each game thereafter. The opening player starts by serving from the right side of the court, hitting the ball diagonally across the net. The server then alternates between left court and right court for each new

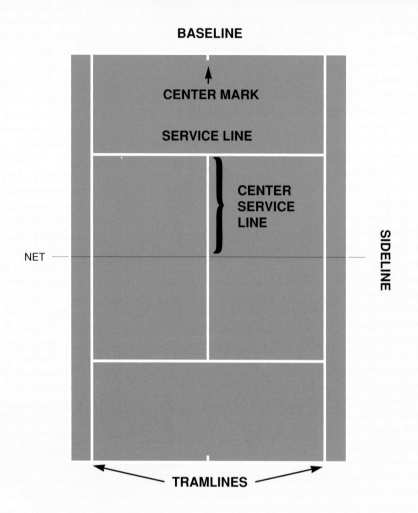

**BASELINE**

CENTER MARK

SERVICE LINE

CENTER SERVICE LINE

NET

SIDELINE

TRAMLINES

point. He or she stands behind the baseline, close to the center mark, and tosses the ball into the air with the hand that is not holding the racket. While the ball is in the air, the racket is brought up and over the head to meet it.

A serve is "good" if it lands in the service court—the box formed by the service line and the net—diagonal to the server. The server is always allowed two serves. This means that if on the first try the ball hits the net or lands out of the service box, which is called a *fault*, the player is allowed a second serve. If the ball nicks the net and then goes into the service court, it is called a *let*, and the server is allowed another first serve. (A foot fault is called if the server steps on or beyond the baseline; this is treated like other faults.) If the player's second serve is also no good, it is called a *double fault*, and the opponent wins the point.

## Ground Strokes

If the service is good and the ball is returned, a rally begins. The service is returned by a shot called a *ground stroke*—any shot hit after the ball has bounced one time. There are two types of ground stroke: the *forehand* and the *backhand*. Both are generally played from the baseline.

The forehand is hit with the front face of the racket. In other words, a right-handed person will hit the ball from the right side of the body; a left-handed person from the left. The forehand is the most commonly played shot in tennis and the one many people find the most comfortable. Steffi Graf uses her expert forehand to attack her opponent. She hits the ball hard and fast and has total control over the ball, allowing her to place it anywhere on the court.

The *backhand* is hit with the back side of the racket; that is, a right-handed person hits the ball from the left side of the body, and vice versa for a left-handed person. This play is awkward for many people, as crossing the arm across the torso to make contact with the ball is not as natural as swinging away from the body. To get a little extra control, many tennis players use a *two-handed backhand*. With this stroke, the left hand is placed above the right (opposite for left-handers) to give support and power.

Many beginners who are frustrated with the backhand find that the two-handed backhand is all they need to master the shot. Says Katie, a 13-year-old player, "I started playing tennis when I was 10, and it was kind of hard to hold the racket. I was okay with the forehand, but I just couldn't get the backhand right. My tennis teacher showed me how to use two hands, and now my backhand is better than my forehand!"

Some of the game's best players have used this technique, including Chris Evert, Jimmy Connors, Tracy Austin, and Bjorn Borg. Monica Seles takes the idea a step further: she is one of the few people to use two hands for both the forehand and the backhand.

The way the racket is held is different for the forehand and the backhand. The eastern forehand grip is also called the "shake hands grip," because a player grasps the racket as though he or she were shaking a person's hand. It is used for the forehand, and beginners often use it for the serve. The eastern backhand grip is counterclockwise from the eastern forehand grip. It sounds tricky to switch grips in the middle of a rally, but it is much more difficult to play a backhand with the wrong grip. A good coach can help a player perfect the grips, and practice makes switching from one to the other a natural part of the game—even in the middle of a tense rally.

Players also need to learn how to get their feet and body into the correct position once they see where the oncoming ball is going to hit the court. If a player's body is not in the right position to execute a stroke, it makes it that much more difficult to return a solid, well-placed shot. The racket should be taken back as soon as possible so there is plenty of time to play the shot without rushing it. It is also important to keep the eyes on the ball until it has been successfully returned across the net.

## Tricky Shots

Other strokes round out a strong player's arsenal. The *volley* is hit before the ball bounces—most frequently close to the net, when it is called a *stop volley*. *Half-volleys* are hit just after the ball has bounced, low and close to the ground. Like ground strokes, all volleys can be hit from either the forehand or the backhand side.

A *lob* is a ball that is directed high into the air, usually to foil an opponent who has advanced to the net to volley. When a player uses the lob, he or she hopes that the ball will go over the other player's head and out of reach. To combat a lob, a competitor uses the *overhead smash*, a stroke hit much like the serve in that the ball is struck from overhead. Played well, the smash is often a powerful winning shot because the fast-moving ball hits hard and bounces out of an opponent's reach.

**The forehand (left) and backhand (right) are both ground strokes. Players cannot let the ball bounce more than once on their side of the net before returning it.**

## Losing Points

Several ways to lose a point are :

- Allowing the ball to bounce twice in your court before returning it.
- Hitting the ball into the net.
- Returning the ball over the net, but out of bounds (hitting the ball "out").
- Hitting the ball more than once in a single stroke.
- Volleying the ball before it has crossed to your side of the net (reaching over the net to get to the ball).

- Allowing the ball to touch any part of your clothing or body besides your racket.
- Allowing you, your racket, or your clothing to touch the net, its supporting posts, or the ground within your opponent's portion of the court.
- Throwing your racket at the ball.

In all professional tournaments and some important amateur events, umpires decide whether a ball has landed "out" or whether it is "good" (landed within the playing court). Most amateur matches, however, are played without an umpire. Players are on the "honor system," and they are expected to agree whether the ball has landed in or out.

Sometimes a player may say that the ball was out, while the opponent insists that it was good. If this happens to you, and the disputed ball is on the other side of the court, give your opponent the benefit of the doubt. After all, he or she was closer to the ball than you were. If this happens too often, however, you may decide to stop playing with a particular opponent. For your own sake, always be honest with your opponents. It isn't much fun to win by cheating.

American John McEnroe won three U.S. Opens and one Wimbledon title during the 1980s.

Throwing a racket after missing a point, cursing, fighting with an opponent or umpire, or deliberately trying to hinder your opponent's ability to hit the ball are all discouraged behavior on the tennis court. For many years, such antics were absolutely forbidden, but in recent years there has been more of this kind of thing—even in professional tennis.

American John McEnroe, a top player in the 1980s, is known not only for his exceptional talent but for his behavior on the court as well. If McEnroe believed a ball was "in" when the umpire called it "out," he would argue, yell, and stomp around the court, disrupting the flow of the game. A bad call might make him hurl his racket, and swear words caused him trouble in more than one tournament.

For a while, amateurs thought such behavior made for a good player. Some even copied it. Steve, a big McEnroe fan says, "We all thought it was really cool to throw our rackets if we played a bad point or act like our opponent was cheating if we didn't like a call he made. But it was really childish, and I think it keeps you from playing your best." Today umpires at amateur and professional events alike have grown stricter, and misconduct can result in points against a player.

## Keeping Score

Tennis is played in *matches*, which are made up of either three or five *sets*. Generally, professional men's singles and doubles are five sets; women's singles, doubles, and mixed doubles are three sets. Sets are made up of *games*. The first player to win six games wins the set, but the player must be ahead by two games. In other words, if the score is tied at 5-5, one player must win two more games in a row to win, making the score 7-5.

For many years, a set could go on for a very long time until one player was finally ahead by two games. For example, in 1968, the first set of a Wimbledon match between Pancho Gonzales and Charlie Pasarell didn't end until the score was 22-24. To solve the problem of extremely long sets, *tie breaks* were introduced. Once a score is 6-6, the first player to win seven points by a margin of at least two wins the tie-break and the set. However, tie breakers are never used in the last set of a match.

Traditionally, it is much easier to win a game when you have the serve. When the receiver wins a game, he or she is said to have "broken" the serve, and this player has a definite advantage in the set. In a tie-breaker, the player who would have served in the next game starts, then the players alternate the serve every two points. In this way no player has an advantage over the other at a crucial time in the match.

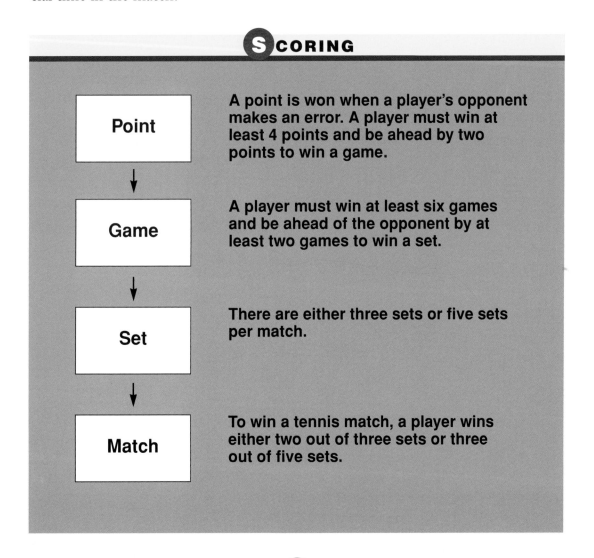

**S**CORING

| Point | A point is won when a player's opponent makes an error. A player must win at least 4 points and be ahead by two points to win a game. |

| Game | A player must win at least six games and be ahead of the opponent by at least two games to win a set. |

| Set | There are either three sets or five sets per match. |

| Match | To win a tennis match, a player wins either two out of three sets or three out of five sets. |

**Martina Navratilova prepares to serve. Concentration and a powerful overhand stroke are needed to send the ball across the court at top speed.**

The scoring used for a tennis game sounds difficult, but it isn't terribly complicated. It is based on the system used in royal tennis, where the number 60 was divided by four, so the points in the game were 15, 30, 45, and 60. Since the word 45 was difficult to say in old French, it was replaced with 40—the same number we use today.

When a game starts, the score is called "love-love." ("Love" means zero in tennis; the term may have originated from an old English saying, "love or nothing.") The first point won by a player is 15, the second is 30, the third is 40, and the next point is game. The server's score is always called out first when announcing the score. Let's say the server has won two points and the opponent has scored one. The score would be 30-15. If the opponent wins the next point, the score is 30-30, or "30 all."

As with a set, a player must win a game by two points, so if both players reach 40, the score of the tied game is called *deuce*. The game will continue until one player has a two-point advantage. Let's say our players are at deuce, but the opponent wins the next point. The score is now said to be "advantage out," or "ad-out"; if the server had won the point, it would be "advantage in," or "ad-in." If the player with the advantage loses the next point, the game goes back to deuce. Until one player wins when he or she has the advantage, the game continues. Confusing? It may sound complicated, but once you start playing, it all falls into place pretty fast.

If you happen to be playing with the sun in your eyes, you'll be happy to learn that your opponent will soon have the same problem. Players change court sides at the completion of the first, third, and alternate games thereafter. By changing sides, neither player has an advantage. An easy way to remember whether it is time to switch sides is to add the set scores of both players together. If the sum is odd, it's time to switch; if it's even, stay where you are. What would you do if the score were 3-2? What would you do if it were 1-3?

## Consistency

As we've learned, points can be won or lost in a variety of ways. Because the serve is the only shot in which a player has complete control over the timing and placement of the ball, a consistent serve is an important part of a winning tennis game. It can give a player a head start by putting the opponent under pressure to return a tough shot at the very start of a point.

If you place a serve so that an opponent cannot reach it, either because it is too fast or too well placed, it is called an *ace*. Boris Becker is well-known for his exceptional serve, and he serves many an ace. His technique allows him to put great power and speed on the ball as it crosses the net, and his consistent success with first serves has often made the difference in whether he wins or loses.

A serve can place a player at an advantage, but it can also do the opposite. If a player has trouble getting the first serve in bounds, it can break the momentum of play. In addition, players traditionally put less power into the second serve to ensure that it goes in. It is very unusual for a second serve to result in an ace. A player gives his or her opponent a free point by double faulting (hitting both serves out), and it is important to make sure that this rarely happens if you are out to win a match.

The first step to success in tennis, as in any sport, is to learn the basics. A good coach can help you get a firm grasp on the techniques and rules of the game, but how do you advance from there? How do you become a competitive player with enough confidence to play in tournaments? We'll try to answer these questions.

**B**ecoming a champion tennis player requires years of proper coaching, conditioning and regular practice against players who are as good or better than you.

# What Does It Take?

**T**ennis can be more than just a way to have fun. Maybe to you, having fun means doing the very best you can at everything you try. There are a lot of reasons why people want to do well in their favorite sport—for one thing, everyone loves to win. The problem is, winning is hard work. If it were easy to be a first-class tennis player, most everyone would be!

There are many things that make a player better than the competition. Some start out with a tremendous amount of talent, but you can be sure that even these lucky few must work hard to achieve their goals. The top professional players spend hours and hours each day with their coaches, going over their weaknesses and practicing the game. That may sound like a pretty good life, but it takes a lot more effort than one might think.

**Tennis matches can be grueling endurance tests, lasting for hours.**

The first thing a player needs is motivation—if it isn't really important to play the best you can, chances are you never will. Most people want to succeed at what they do, but not everyone is willing to put in the hours of hard work it takes to be the best.

Think of it like this: for a lot of students, getting an "A" on a test is not important—just getting a passing grade is acceptable. Therefore, they will study only enough to make sure they don't flunk. But a "C" or "B" isn't good enough for some students; a grade has to be an "A" or they feel like they have failed. There is no question that it is easier for some students to get good grades than others, but every student has to study hard to do their best. The ones who really excel are those who want a good grade so much that they are willing to really work for it. This is what we call motivation.

Can people learn motivation? No one knows for sure. Usually motivation is a natural drive and comes from within. If you really love tennis, chances are you'll be motivated to do well. If you don't love the game, it will be hard to put forth the effort it takes to succeed. People always do better at things they enjoy.

Coaches can help create the drive to succeed in players who have a lot of natural talent but a tendency to be lazy. An encouraging partner is also a plus. Having a friend who motivates you to play often and with whom you enjoy playing can make even the hard work seem fun. Joining a team that expects you to do your best for the good of the team is another way to build motivation, since players want to keep up with their teammates and succeed in competitive play.

Setting goals can help, too. For example, maybe you have an inconsistent first serve. Spend time trying to improve it. Set a series of goals. Tell yourself that at the end of two weeks, you will be able to hit five good serves in a row. When you reach that goal, set another. Once you achieve a strong first serve, you can reward yourself—perhaps by playing in a tournament or buying a new piece of equipment.

As you practice a certain number of hours each week and work to reach your goals, you'll see a big improvement in your game. After a while, you may find that you *want* to spend a lot of time sharpening your skills. Gone will be the days when you had to force yourself to get out on the court.


## Practice

No one becomes good at anything without practice. In the early stages of learning the game of tennis, practicing won't always be fun. You'll find yourself practicing the service toss over and over, learning how to hold the racket correctly, practicing strokes without a ball, running laps around the court, and a variety of other things that may not seem like a good way to spend your time. As you get a little better, however, practice gets to be more and more fast-paced. The harder you work in the beginning, the quicker you'll find yourself having fun on the court.

Many tennis champions learned to play when they were still very young. Practice is everything, but a little natural talent helps, too.

Gripping the tennis racket properly is a skill that 1993 Wimbledon champion Pete Sampras can't take for granted.

Practicing with friends, on a team, with a coach, or even by yourself are all excellent ways to improve your skills. If you can't find anyone who wants to play, you can practice your serve alone. Bring a bucket of balls to the court and fire away!

There are other ways to practice by yourself. Many tennis courts have practice walls, which have a line painted on them at the height where the top of the net would be. Just hit the ball against the wall, returning it after it has bounced once. If you can't get to a tennis court, hit the ball against a wall at your school, or fire some serves at your parents' garage door. Not only will this give you good practice on the best form for your ground strokes and serve, but it will help you learn to judge where the ball will go if it is hit in a certain way or at a certain speed. You can even draw a circle on the wall and practice hitting the ball directly to that spot. This will teach you how to place the ball.

When you practice, you have the chance to make the motion and technique of any shot seem natural to you so that when you're playing a match, you won't have to think about whether you are doing everything correctly. Here are a few things to think about when you're practicing:

- Are you using the right grip for the shot?
- Are you keeping your wrist firm?
- Are you keeping your eye on the ball?
- Is your body in the right position to hit the shot?
- When you move around the court, are you keeping your balance?

Your tennis coach can tell you exactly what you need to know to hit all of your shots correctly and powerfully. With a little practice, you are sure to master them. Even watching a professional tennis match on television is a form of practice. Seeing how the best players hit their shots is a sure way to refine your own style.

Many players are especially gifted at the game. Their natural abilities are astounding, and their practice time makes them that much better. Legend has it that Arthur Ashe discovered Yannick Noah hitting a ball around a playground with a stick. Recognizing Noah's tremendous athletic ability, excellent hand-eye coordination, and superior strength, Ashe encouraged him to take up tennis and made sure he began a strict practice schedule. Noah may have had a lot of talent to begin with, but without hard work and dedication he would not have become the great player he is.

## Concentration

The best players all share one very important thing: a strong ability to focus. This means a player concentrates so intensely on the game, that nothing is able to distract him or her from putting out the best possible effort.

Monica Seles is said to have one great advantage: her mind. Nothing can distract her on the court, and even after long hours of practice, she is still thinking about the game. Her coaches have remarked that as a young player of 12 years old she could practice for six or seven hours without losing concentration. She could go months without playing a tournament and still stay interested in the game.

Concentration is often a natural talent, but it can be improved with a little effort. Like mastering the game of tennis, it takes practice. If your mind starts to wander while you're playing, bring it back into focus by thinking your way through the shots. Don't get distracted or lose your temper. If you've made an unforced error, don't dwell on it—move on to the next point with a fresh attitude.

Many people are nervous before a big match. Spend a little bit of time relaxing before you start to play. Clear your mind, take some deep breaths, and focus on the match. Try to prepare yourself by knowing your opponent's weaknesses. If you take advantage of them, you'll play well. Remember that your opponent is probably nervous, too. Instead of dwelling on your nerves, try to take advantage of your opponent's similar situation.

Most important, keep your mind on the match. If you're tired, don't let yourself think about it. If you're angry about a call your opponent made, forget about it. Get on to the next point.

## Fitness

A key ingredient to athletic success is physical fitness. A match can last a long time, and if you are not in shape, your opponent has a definite advantage. Players like Jim Courier and Martina Navratilova succeed not only because of their exceptional talent, but because they are in such great shape. As their opponents begin to wear out, Courier and Navratilova can keep going.

To increase endurance, many tennis players run as a regular part of their training. It is a good way to build stamina and speed. Drills can help increase agility. The shuttle sprint, for example, improves the way players turn and move on the court. Three balls are placed on the singles sidelines, four or five inches apart. A player stands behind the opposite sideline, sprints across the court and picks up one ball, then sprints back and puts the ball down. This is repeated until all three balls are retrieved. As players get into shape, they can increase the number of balls.

To build strength, some players lift weights. Others do a variety of exercises like push-ups, sit-ups, and squats. Coaches offer important information about building strength, teaching a player to start slowly and never do anything that could cause an injury. Whether you are running, lifting weights, or doing shuttle sprints, don't try to do too much too soon. Start out slowly and do some stretching exercises before you begin. Stretch after you are done as well.

A lot of things come together to make a superior player. You can overcome your weaknesses with practice, you can use a friend or a coach to get yourself motivated and help you concentrate, and you can work out to build your strength. In the end, you will have control over how good a game you play. Whether or not you win is up to you.

**The powerful backhand stroke has made Jim Courier one of the top-seeded players in the world of tennis.**

**TENNIS GEAR**

**Visors and caps are more popular these days to keep off the hot sun.**

**Proper grip size of the racket handle is necessary for control.**

**Lightweight clothing is important for comfort.**

**Tennis shoes are designed specifically for fast starts and stops on the court surfaces.**

**C**ombining your strengths with that of another player, and learning to volley against two opponents, makes doubles a fun variation on the game of tennis.

# Getting Involved

## CHAPTER FIVE

**F**ortunately, tennis is a popular sport, and it is easy to get involved. There are many clubs and teams available all around the United States, and most of them are eager to accept new players. How do you find the one best suited for you?

As we've already learned, coaches or teachers are vital to playing your best game of tennis. Not only will they teach you the techniques of the game, but they can help you get involved in tournament play and help you recognize and fight your weaknesses. Beginners don't generally need a private coach, so they can start with lessons at a local club or recreation center.

Many communities offer tennis lessons through their recreation departments. For little or no money, you can join a class with other students who also want to learn to play tennis. Some classes even provide beginners with tennis rackets so they have a chance to learn the game before buying their own equipment.

Anyone who is just starting out will benefit from spending time with a knowledgeable teacher. Not only will you learn the fine points of tennis, you'll find your confidence growing as well. A good teacher will also make sure you are exercising properly to avoid injury and help keep you motivated. Once you've learned the basics, you might want to take part in smaller classes or even try private lessons. Your community's recreation department, a physical education teacher at school, or a state tennis association can help you find a good coach.

Younger students, aged ten and under, can also start by playing what is called "short tennis." In this game, players use half the court with a shorter net strung across it. Shorter, lighter rackets are used so that young people can have a good time and learn the basics of the game without having to cover the distance of a regulation court. Short tennis can also be played indoors, so players in cold climates can practice in the winter before trying the real game in the spring when the weather has improved. YMCAs around the country teach kids the game of short tennis with the hope of getting them interested in the sport at an early age.

**Many schools and athletic organizations offer tennis classes for young people. Take advantage of one and see if tennis is a game you'll want to enjoy for a lifetime.**

The USTA has started a school program that introduces tennis to children in physical education classes—another good way to learn the basics. Students who are particularly interested in the sport are told how to get involved outside of school.

Legendary pro Arthur Ashe started the National Junior Tennis League (NJTL), an organization that introduces the game to young people of all backgrounds, whether rich or poor. Players who can't afford to pay for tennis lessons or buy a racket can still join the NJTL and play the game. Ashe wanted youngsters to have the chance to participate in the sport and to learn how to deal with competition. Each year tournaments are sponsored through this organization.

Many tennis clubs have excellent programs for young tennis players. Not only are lessons and courts available to members, but club teams play matches against other clubs. Coaches can help players learn about tournaments sponsored by the USTA or state tennis associations and prepare them for competition. You can find out about tennis clubs near your home by contacting the USTA or looking in your local telephone directory under "Tennis Instruction."

If you aren't comfortable starting out in tournament play all by yourself, there are other options. Find a partner and start out in doubles matches. Perhaps your serve is strong, but you have a weak volley. Find a player who can bring a tough volley to your partnership. You may find that not only do you win matches, but your volley will improve with a talented partner. Playing doubles is not only a good way to get into the spirit of competition, it is also a lot of fun.

School and community teams also offer a good introduction to competition. Most high schools have tennis teams that compete against other schools.

---

### Rolling Hills Tennis Club
### Girl's Ladder

| **A**<br>13-14 | **B**<br>13-14 |
|---|---|
| Jenny | Debra |
| Linda | Diedre |
| Chelsea | Beth |
| Kaitlan | |
| Maria | |

### Rolling Hills Tennis Club
### Boy's Ladder

| **A**<br>13-14 | **B**<br>13-14 |
|---|---|
| Tom | Jeremy |
| Craig | Charlie |
| John | Sam |
| Rick | |
| Michael | |

Here is a ladder for the 13- and 14-year-old players at an imaginary club. The club only has five places on its A Ladder.

Jenny is the best female player in her age group, but if Kaitlan—who is the number four player on her ladder—challenges her and wins, she will be the number one player on the A Ladder, and Jenny will move into second place. Maria, who is at the bottom of the A Ladder, will move to the top of the B Ladder because there are only five spaces on the A Ladder.

Sam is the number three player on the boy's B Ladder, but if he challenges Michael and wins, he will take the fifth place on the male ladder in his age group. Michael will move to the number one spot on the B Ladder.

What happens if Diedre challenges Debra and wins? If Charlie challenges Rick and wins?

# Glossary

**Ace.** A serve that is either too fast or out of reach, winning the server a point.

**Amateur.** Someone who plays a sport but is not paid money to do so.

**Backhand.** A ground stroke hit with the back face of the racket; that is, a right-handed person hits it from the left side of the body, and vice versa for a left-handed person.

**Baselines.** The lines at the ends of the court. If a ball bounces beyond these lines, it is considered out of bounds.

**Deuce.** When opponents are tied at 40 points each in a game.

**Double fault.** A lost point as the result of two missed serves.

**Doubles.** A tennis match between four players, with teams of two people competing against each other.

**Fault.** A serve that cannot be played because it is either out or hits the net.

**Forehand.** The ground stroke hit with the front face of the racket; that is, a right-handed person hits it from the right side of the body, and vice versa for a left-handed person.

**Game.** A series of at least four points, with one person serving every point to his or her opponent. A player must win a game by at least two points.

**Grand Slam.** The honor of winning the four major professional tennis tournaments in one year. These events include the Australian Open, The Championships (Wimbledon), the French Open, and the U.S. Open.

**Ground stroke.** A shot hit after the ball has bounced once.

**Half-volley.** A stroke hit just after the ball bounces, low and close to the ground.

***Jeu de paume.*** The earliest known form of tennis, this game was played indoors at French monasteries during the eleventh century.

**Lawn tennis.** The name given to the sport of tennis by the British in the nineteenth century. The English still use this name today.

**Lob.** A stroke that hits the ball into the air, usually above the head of an opponent who is at the net to volley.

**Match.** A series of the best of three or the best of five sets in tennis.

**Overhead smash.** A stroke hit with the ball overhead that uses a motion similar to that of the serve.

# For Additional Information

**The United States Tennis Association** and the **Canadian Tennis Association** can give you additional information about tennis, as well as assist you in finding a good coach or club. They can also give you the phone number of your state or province's tennis association.

**USTA**
1212 Avenue of the Americas, 12th Floor
New York, NY 10036
(212) 302-3322

**Canadian Tennis Association**
3111 Steeles Avenue West
Downsview, Ontario M3J 3H2
CANADA

Other books about tennis include
*Play the Game: Tennis* by Simon Lee, Ward Lock Ltd., 1988.
*Improve your Tennis Skills* by Anita Ganeri, Usborne Publishing Ltd., 1989.

# *Index*

Agassi, Andre, 13
Ashe, Arthur, 37, 43
Austin, Tracy, 25
Australian Open, 9-10

Becker, Boris, 31
Borg, Bjorn, 25
Borotra, Jean, 9
Brugnon, Jaques, 9
Bruguera, Sergi, 16
Budge, Don, 10

Capriati, Jennifer, 10
Chang, Michael, 7
Cochet, Henri, 9
Connors, Jimmy, 25
Courier, Jim, 16, 38
Court, Margaret, 10

Davis Cup, 9

Edberg, Stefan, 10
Evert, Chris, 25

French Open, 7, 9, 16

Gonzales, Pancho, 29
Grand Slam, 10

Lacoste, Rene, 9
Laver, Rod, 10
Lendl, Ivan, 16
Lenglen, Suzanne, 10

McEnroe, John, 28

National Junior Tennis League (NJTL), 43
Navratilova, Martina, 38
Noah, Yannick, 13, 37

O'Connolly, Maureen, 10

Pasarell, Charlie, 29

Sampras, Pete, 16
Seles, Monica, 7, 10, 13, 25

tennis
    amateur vs. professional, 10
    balls, 20
    challenge system, 9
    classes, 41-44
    clothing, 20
    court(s)
    dimensions, 17-18
    surfaces, 15-16
    ground strokes, 25-26
    history of, 7-10
    introduced to the U.S., 8
    lawn, 8
    learning, 5, 33-39, 41-44
    meaning of the name, 7
    open tournaments, 10-13
    rackets, 18-19
    rallies, 23
    rules of play, 23-28
    scoring, 28-31

United States Tennis Association (USTA), 9,
    12, 43
U.S. Open, 9

Wimbledon, 8, 9, 10, 16, 20, 29
Wingfield, Maj. Walter Clopton, 8, 16